We Are Important

By Amulya Veldanda Vadali
Illustrated by Artificial Intelligence

Discussion Questions

1) Do you know what job you want to do when you grow up?

2) What are some of the challenges you may face?

3) Why is that job important?

4) Think about the people you interact with every day. It could be a teacher, bus driver, or someone else. What are some of the challenges they may deal with in their jobs?

5) How does their job affect your life?

6) How would your life be affected if they weren't doing their job?

7) Do you think computers are important? Why or why not?

8) List some of the ways that you use computers. (Ex: to play games, study, write stories, etc)

9) Look back at your answer to Question 1. Can you think of any ways that computers may help you in your future job?

Author's Note

Hi all! Thank you for taking the time to read my book. All images in this book were created by an AI illustration tool called DALL-E. I know this is a controversial topic, so I wanted to mention that this was just a fun experiment. I was intrigued to see if it would even be possible to illustrate a whole children's book using this tool. And while it is possible, I saw that there are many limitations to using AI in this capacity. So, I will be sticking with traditional illustrators for my other series. That being said, I do believe that computers and AI will play a significant role in our future. The challenge going forward will be to find the proper balance between human creativity and the efficiency of computers. I do believe we will reach that balance as we learn and evolve.

Visit www.avvbooks.com if you would like to submit an occupation suggestion for the next book! Also, please leave a review, follow us on social media, and share! Thank you!

Website: www.avvbooks.com
Instagram @amulyavv_books

This book was fully illustrated using an Artificial Intelligence tool called DALL-E. DALL-E was trained by software engineers to draw unique illustrations from text captions inputted by the user.

In simple terms, each picture in this book was drawn by a computer program in less than a minute!

There was once a dog who had a dream. Her dedication to science was a bit extreme. At a young age, she found a lab coat and some safety glasses too. And she started on her way to discover something new. Every day, she would go to her lab and try to learn. It was late in the evening before she would return. She would ask a question and search for the answer. Her goal was to find a cure for a disease such as cancer. She would mix different chemicals, and her glasses would fog. Then, she would quickly jot down some notes in her observation log. Everyone tried to tell her it would be a hard job to do. That made it even more exciting from her point of view. As a scientist, she had the potential to help many dogs in need. That was her motivation to work hard and succeed!

Later in the year, the scientist decided to expand her lab and get it redesigned. So, she went out and hired the best architect she could find. This dog's job was to creatively design the new place. She would address all her client's needs while making the best use of the space. The architect soon put together a detailed floor plan, which included every window and door. She even specified what materials would be used for the counters and the floor. In addition, the architect had to know all the township building codes and laws. And she constantly had to be observant to catch any serious design flaws.

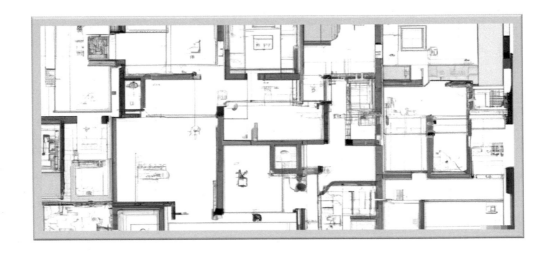

The most important part of the architect's job was communicating with her client. She always tried her best to meet every request, no matter how giant. Some clients expected far too much in too little time and didn't want to spend even one extra dime. Her last client, for example, had asked for tiles that needed to be imported from far away. But then he got upset and angry when there was a construction delay. She had to talk to him calmly to make him understand. "Things don't always go just as they're planned."

Our architect had a former colleague who now worked at a school. He taught fifth-grade math, and he had only one rule. "Never look at a problem and say you can't figure it out. You can solve anything you approach without a doubt." His passion for math inspired the kids to give it a try. They did algebra and geometry and even memorized 20 digits of pi.

The teacher knew that math wasn't always a yummy piece of cake. He never barked if a student made a silly mistake. He had been in their shoes not so long ago. He understood it took time and practice to learn and grow! But he loved to teach because he knew one thing. He inspired the pups he took under his wing! Their confidence showed when they walked out the door to sixth grade. One day, they would do great things, and he would be proud of the part he played.

One of the teacher's students went on to lead the first crew to Mars. Up past the sky and moon and out toward the stars. This dog was an astronaut who loved to be out in space. He was heading to Mars with a team to set up a base. As the leader, he had to ensure they stayed on the right path. He regularly needed to use his knowledge of physics and math!

The team's job was to reach Mars, settle down, and look around. They wanted to see if they could grow plants in the ground. They would search for rich minerals and other life forms and check for dangerous conditions or sudden storms. Our astronaut's job was to assess if Mars could ever be a good place to stay. Just in case dogs ever wanted to leave earth and move far away. All the collected data would lead to a better understanding of space, time, and more. He was helping future generations by risking his life to explore.

Ninety-five million miles away, back on earth, another dog was exploring space and time by looking at old bones. This archaeologist loved to dig through the dirt, looking for skeletons, ancient artifacts, and stones. His role was to understand the dogs of the past. The history of the earth was rich and vast.

He often heard from his peers that archaeology was a dying field of study. They thought his passion for searching through the dirt was just plain nutty. But he loved what he did, and he had found many fascinating things; old cloth, yellow parchment, and some gold that belonged to the kings. Every day, he learned about ancient cultures and determined how early generations had lived and died. The history, traditions, and natural disasters of the past could not be denied. He truly believed the experiences of our ancestors could teach us how to better adapt. There was valuable information there in the ground waiting to be tapped!

We explored the future of space exploration and the stories of the past, but now we will go in between. There was a dog doing his job to keep our present world clean. Every week, he rushed around town to pick up all the trash in time. Sometimes he had to deal with open bins, stinky foods, and slime. Others often didn't see how important his job was for the town. But they would soon realize it if their garbage was piling up all around. It was a job that needed to be done without delay every week, or every house in every street would soon begin to reek!

The role needed someone strong and fit, with good stamina and comfortable shoes. And most importantly, someone tolerant of messy folks and smelly ooze. And even with all the trash collector faced, he was rarely appreciated for his work. Instead, he was often ignored, judged, or just given a smirk. But the next week, he would still be there without a second thought. He's one dog that everyone in town would always rely on a lot!

Our trash collector often found many items in the garbage bins. Common findings included rotten, old sweet potato skins. Those potatoes came from a farmer out in the fields. He worked hard daily to maintain his crop yields. First, he checked if the soil had the necessary nutrients for plants. He then inspected the ground for mice and other pests, like beetles and ants. After planting the sprouts, he ensured they were getting water and sun. Then, he harvested the crops once the growing period was done. The sweet potatoes were next sent all over the country to markets and stores. And from there, they would be bought and would soon reach all our kitchen drawers. Without the farmers, there would be no crops to eat. There would be no sweet potato for breakfast, lunch, dinner, or even a yummy treat. The farmer knew all this, so he did his work with pride. He would continue to do his job and send his sweet potatoes far and wide.

One day, while the farmer was working, he cut his paws badly on some wire. He ignored the injury for a few days, but the cuts soon began to burn like fire. So, he left the farm to see the doctor in town. She inspected his paws with a small frown. "You should have come in sooner," the doctor said, "these cuts are clearly infected because they're inflamed and red." She cleaned the wounds and wrapped them with fresh bandages and gauze. Then, she prescribed him some antibiotic cream to apply to his paws.

After tending to the wounds, the doctor completed the farmer's physical check-up for the year. She listened to his heart, checked his blood pressure, and gave him the "all clear." The doctor had gone to school for many years to become an expert in her field. She took care of all her patients until they were completely healed. Whether it was a cut, cold, or cramp, she always knew what to do. She could leave her patients feeling almost as good as new.

After a long day at the office, our doctor wanted to sit down to dine. She stopped by her favorite café because the food was divine! Immediately, the waitress came by and brought her a drink. She then gave the doctor time to look at the menu and think. The doctor ordered a sweet potato soup and some bread. She then scarfed down her food, drove home, and went to bed.

The waitress was also exhausted after working a very long day. She had run back and forth, writing down orders and taking plates away. She would have liked to sit down for a while to put up her feet. But there were still dogs coming in, ready to eat. So, she put on a smile and did her job. It didn't matter if a customer was a jerk or a snob. She always made sure every dog left the café with a full belly. That's the work that waitresses do, whether in a café, restaurant, or deli.

One day in the café, a major fire started in the oven. The firefighter was there at the click of a button. He quickly made sure everyone was safely out of the way. Then, he put out the fire without delay. Due to the speed of his actions, there was minimal damage to the café. The owner was shocked and grateful to see that everything was okay.

This firefighter also frequently fought forest fires that traveled quickly through the trees. These were becoming more common because of climate change and the additional degrees. Warmer temperatures resulted in drier soil across the forest floor. This led to the formation of larger and more dangerous fires than before. Despite that, this dog would don his gear and go out to fight the flame. He would do this for the environment and his community, not for money or fame. In his free time, he also visited local schools to teach pups how to stop, drop, and roll. Keeping the public safe was his primary goal!

After a hard day out in the forest, our firefighter liked to stop at the park. There was often a local musician there that would play her guitar and bark. The firefighter would hum along, tap his paw, and do a little sway. The music always helped him relax after a tiring and stressful day.

The musician's parents had first told her that singing would not be a suitable career. But she was passionate and very talented; it soon became clear. She put her heart into her music every night and was soon discovered by a major record label, to her delight. She was now quite famous and had fans across the world. But she still loved to play in her hometown, where her talent had first unfurled. In many ways, her music brought the whole community closer. Everyone came out to listen, from the mayor to the grocer! After her performance, the musician was excited to share that she was soon leaving for her first European tour. Instead of saying hello to her crowd, she would soon be saying bonjour!

That brings us to the end of this story. We saw many jobs in all their glory. Each one was just as crucial to society as the next. All the dogs were out there in the world just trying to do their best. We must always take pride in the jobs that we do. And never forget that others are just as important too!

The software engineer's job involved writing codes, building algorithms, and solving puzzles. He wanted to use computers to help dogs handle common daily troubles. But, if computers became too intelligent, wouldn't they take over all the work there was to do? In that case, what jobs would be left behind for actual dogs like me and you? The software engineer insisted there was no need to stress. "Computers may be able to draw, count, and sing, but they will never be able to use common sense. It is impossible for them to think creatively or decide their own goals. For that, they will always need someone behind their controls."

Used the right way, computers could be powerful tools to help dogs succeed. They could allow dogs in all different fields to improve their efficiency and speed. For example, a computer could help our scientist do a time-consuming task like counting cells on a plate. Then, she would have much more time to think, research, and discover something great. Perhaps soon, dogs and computers would work together side by side. That is the future this software engineer hoped to provide.

A journalist soon came to interview the Captain about his flying career. She had a list of questions to ask and a few doubts to clear. Rather than just reporting on dates and facts, she was interested in sharing what the Captain was feeling. Her primary goal was to convey every emotion her subject was revealing. The journalist took her job very seriously because she knew she had the power to inform. A journalist's words could lead to revolution and reform. For this reason, she needed to be able to separate fact from fiction. And, of course, she needed creativity, good grammar, and perfect diction!

After the interview, the journalist sat at her desk and reviewed her notes. She highlighted essential facts and underlined direct quotes. She was about to start writing her article when she suddenly received a text. Now she knew what story she would be chasing next! A lead had just emerged about a software engineer using computers to help others get their work done. This dog believed that the age of technology had only just begun. This topic was controversial because dogs everywhere feared computers would one day take their jobs. The journalist knew a story like this could lead to panic and angry mobs!

Soon the musician left to catch her plane for her music tour of France. She got to meet and shake paws with the Captain in advance. Dogs everywhere now wanted to travel more than ever because they were tired of being home. The virus had kept dogs inside for two years, and now they wanted to roam. But there was a significant pilot shortage in the nation, which could be explained. It was due to COVID, early pilot retirement, and the long time it took to be trained.

Despite all that, this pilot had been flying for many years. He knew everything about planes, from the engines to the gears. Along with all his knowledge, he also had traits that helped him fly. He was confident and calm and knew what to do if there was ever an emergency in the sky. In addition to that, he was able to communicate clearly and work well with his crew. And even after so many years of flying every day, he still enjoyed the view!